BEHIND THE CURTAIN
Act Out History's BIGGEST Dramas

FIRE AND BRIMSTONE

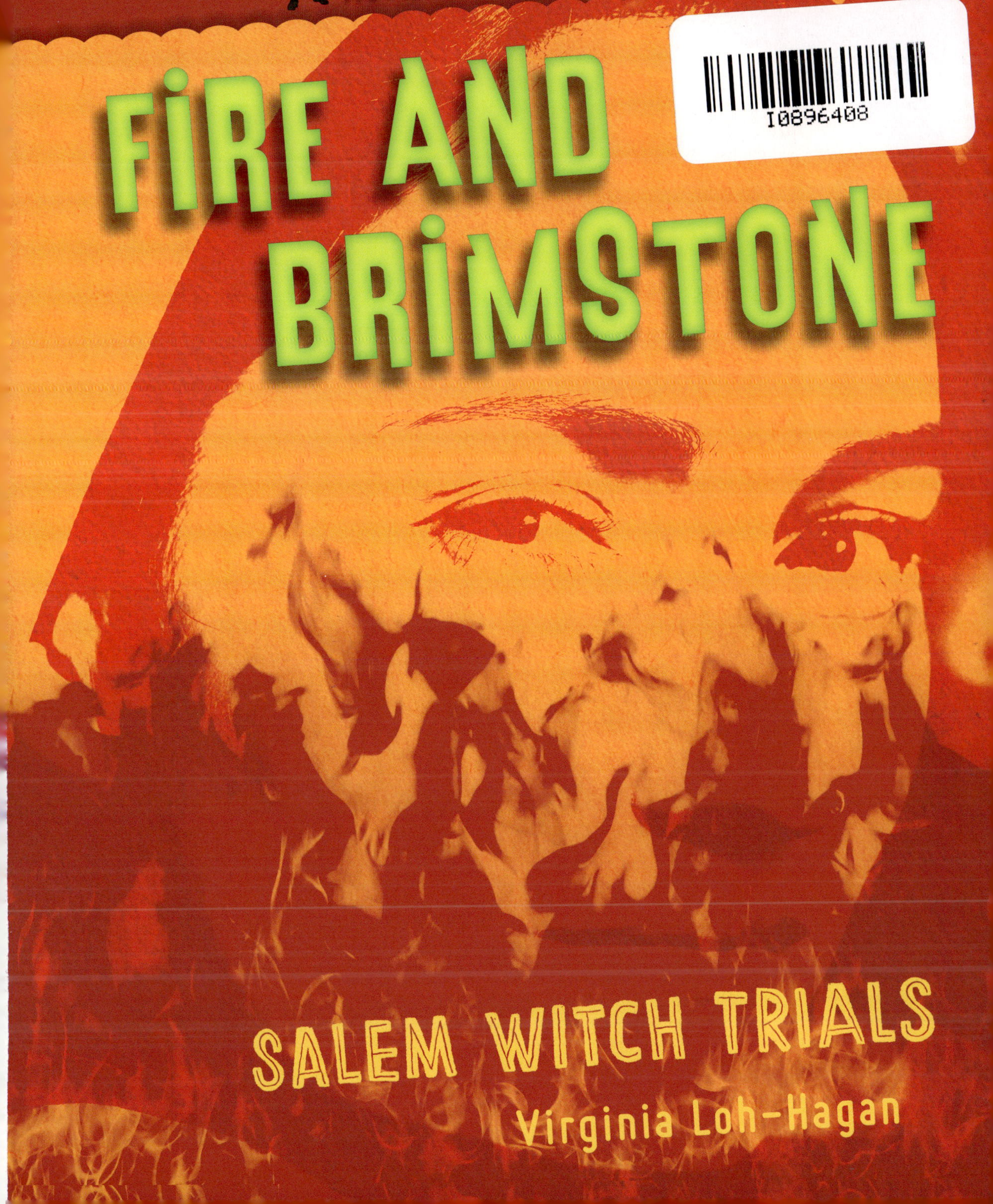

SALEM WITCH TRIALS

Virginia Loh-Hagan

45TH PARALLEL PRESS

Published in the United States of America by Cherry Lake Publishing
Ann Arbor, Michigan
www.cherrylakepublishing.com

Reading Adviser: Marla Conn, MS, Ed., Literacy specialist, Read-Ability Inc.
Cover Designer: Felicia Macheske

Photo Credits: © Irina Salmankhanova/Shutterstock.com, cover, 1; © Hols/Shutterstock.com, 5; © Jessica Bauman/Shutterstock.com, 6; © Armin Staudt/Shutterstock.com, 11; © F_N/Shutterstock.com, 17; © Zolotarevs/Shutterstock.com, 18; © Everett Historical/Shutterstock.com, 21, 25, 29; © Devin Meijer/Shutterstock.com, 22

Graphic Elements Throughout: © Chipmunk131/Shutterstock.com; © Nowik Sylwia/Shutterstock.com; © Andrey_Popov/Shutterstock.com; © NadzeyaShanchuk/Shutterstock.com; © KathyGold/Shutterstock.com; © Black creator/Shutterstock.com; © Edvard Molnar/Shutterstock.com; © Elenadesign/Shutterstock.com; © estherpoon/Shutterstock.com

45th Parallel Press is an imprint of Cherry Lake Publishing.

Library of Congress Cataloging-in-Publication Data

Names: Loh-Hagan, Virginia, author.
Title: Fire and Brimstone : Salem Witch Trials / Virginia Loh-Hagan.
Description: Ann Arbor, Michigan : Cherry Lake Publishing, [2020]. | Series: Behind the Curtain | Includes index.
Identifiers: LCCN 2019032924 (print) | LCCN 2019032925 (ebook) | ISBN 9781534159457 (hardcover) | ISBN 9781534161757 (paperback) | ISBN 9781534160606 (pdf) | ISBN 9781534162907 (ebook)
Subjects: LCSH: Trials (Witchcraft)–Massachusetts–Salem–History–17th century–Juvenile literature.
Classification: LCC KFM2478.8.W5 L64 2020 (print) | LCC KFM2478.8.W5 (ebook) | DDC 133.4/3097445–dc23
LC record available at https://lccn.loc.gov/2019032924
LC ebook record available at https://lccn.loc.gov/2019032925

Cherry Lake Publishing would like to acknowledge the work of the Partnership for 21st Century Learning, a Network of Battelle for Kids. Please visit *http://www.battelleforkids.org/networks/p21* for more information.

Printed in the United States of America
Corporate Graphics

A Note on Dramatic Retellings

Participating in Readers Theater, or dramatic retellings, can greatly improve reading skills, especially fluency. The books in the **BEHIND THE CURTAIN** series give readers opportunities to learn about important historical events in a fun and engaging way. These books serve as a bridge to more complex texts. All the characters are real figures from history; however, their stories have been fictionalized. To learn more about the people and the events, check out the Viewpoints and Perspectives series and the Perspectives Library series, as the **BEHIND THE CURTAIN** books are aligned to these stories.

TABLE of CONTENTS

HISTORICAL BACKGROUND

The Salem witch **trials** began in February 1692. They lasted until May 1693. This happened in Salem Village, Massachusetts. At this time, people believed in witches. They lived hard lives. They feared attacks from Native Americans. They were mistrustful of each other.

Betty Parris and Abigail Williams were young girls. They began having fits. They made weird body movements. They screamed. A doctor said they were under a witch's spell. They accused several local women of **witchcraft**.

Soon, people started to panic. More young girls said they were taken over by witches. They accused more women of being witches.

FLASH FACT!

People wrote books about witch hunting.

Vocabulary

trials (TRYE-uhlz) formal examinations of evidence in a court

witchcraft (WICH-kraft) the practice of witch magic

FLASH FACT!

As many as 80,000 suspected witches were executed in Europe between 1500 and 1660.

Vocabulary

tried (TRYED) had a trial

convicted (kuhn-VIKT-id) charged as guilty

executed (EK-suh-kyoot-id) put to death

A special court was set up. It was called the Court of Oyer and Terminer. Oyer means to hear. Terminer means to decide.

In June 1692, Bridget Bishop was the first to be **tried** and **convicted** of witchcraft. She was **executed**. She was hung on Gallows Hill.

Over 200 men, women, and children were accused of witchcraft. Up to 150 people were found guilty. Over 45 people confessed. There were 14 women and 5 men executed. Some people died in jail. One man was crushed to death by stones. The Salem witch trials were the result of the deadliest witch hunt in U.S. history.

CAST of CHARACTERS

NARRATOR: person who helps tell the story

BETTY PARRIS: a 9-year-old girl from Salem Village who says she was attacked by a witch

JOHN BARROWE: a **minister** from Salem Town who hears about the evil in Salem Village

TITUBA: a young slave girl from Barbados who is accused of being a witch

PATIENCE DOD: a woman accused of being a witch

MARTHA SMART: a girl who lives in Salem Village and accuses others of being witches

BACKSTORY
SPOTLIGHT BIOGRAPHY

Goodwife "Goody" Ann Glover was called the "last witch of Boston." She was killed in 1688. She was the last person to be hanged in Boston, Massachusetts, as a witch. Glover and her daughter were immigrants from Ireland. They worked as housekeepers for the Goodwin family. Martha Goodwin was 13 years old. She accused Glover's daughter of stealing laundry. Glover argued with Martha. Martha soon became ill and began acting strangely. A doctor said Martha was affected by witchcraft. Glover was arrested. She was accused of being a witch. She could not be understood because she spoke Gaelic. People said she was speaking the devil's language. Dolls were found at her house. People said these were witch tools. They might have been saints. In 1988, the Boston City Council set November 16 as Goody Glover Day.

Vocabulary

minister (MIN-ih-stur)
a leader of a church

FLASH FACT!

Betty Parris's father was Reverend Samuel Parris. He was the minister of Salem Village.

ACT 1

NARRATOR: *It's 1692. Something odd is happening in Salem Village.* **JOHN BARROWE** *comes to Salem Village. He has received an urgent letter. He speaks with little* **BETTY PARRIS***.*

BETTY: You're a long way from home. Salem Town is several miles away. What are you doing here?

JOHN: Your father sent me an **urgent** letter. He asked me to come check things out. He said you and your cousin, Abigail, are not well.

BETTY: We're **afflicted**. We have terrible **fits**. We have no control. We scream. Our bodies twist into strange positions.

JOHN: Anything else?

BETTY: We have bites and pinches. They're on our arms and legs.

JOHN: Have you seen a doctor?

BETTY: Yes, Father sent for a doctor.

JOHN: What did the doctor say?

Vocabulary

urgent (UR-juhnt) very important and needing immediate attention

afflicted (uh-FLIK-tid) suffering or troubled

fits (FITS) shaking attacks

FLASH FACT!

Church members prayed for the afflicted girls.

BETTY: The doctor said there was nothing he could do. He couldn't find anything wrong with our bodies.

JOHN: That means this is **spiritual**. It must be the devil's work.

BETTY: That makes sense. This started when Abigail and I went to see Tituba last week.

JOHN: Who is Tituba?

BETTY: She is a slave. She works for our family.

JOHN: What happened?

BETTY: She dropped an egg white into a glass of water. The egg white sank into the water. Then, we saw a **coffin** in the glass.

JOHN: Then what?

BETTY: Oh, it's just so terrible! I can't talk about it anymore!

NARRATOR: *Betty goes into one of her fits.* **JOHN BARROWE** *goes to see* **TITUBA***.*

JOHN: What happened with you and Betty and Abigail?

TITUBA: The girls wanted me to **predict** their future.

JOHN: Did you?

TITUBA: Of course not. I know that fortune-telling is a crime. It's also a sin in our community. Only God can predict the future.

Vocabulary

spiritual (SPIR-ih-choo-uhl) not of the natural world

coffin (KAW-fin) case for a dead body

predict (prih-DIKT) to make a guess

FLASH FACT!

The girls accused Tituba of being a witch.

JOHN: Well, the girls said you did. They said they saw a coffin in the glass.

TITUBA: Is that why the girls are in **hysterics**?

JOHN: We believe the girls are under a witch's spell. The devil uses witches to do bad things.

TITUBA: So you're saying I'm a witch?

JOHN: Your actions have brought **disease** and **despair**. People are sick. Crops have failed. These are all signs of the devil's work.

NARRATOR: *Several more girls are in hysterics. They accuse more people of being witches. Salem Village is in an uproar.* **TITUBA** *and* **PATIENCE DOD** *are talking.*

PATIENCE: Everyone has lost their minds. Why are they believing these girls and not us?

LOCATION SHOOTING
REAL-WORLD SETTING

Salem is in the Massachusetts Bay area. It's a little north of Boston. It started as a fishing and farming area. The Native Americans called it Naumkeag. This means "fishing place." In 1692, there were 2 main areas. One is Salem Village. It was a farming area. It was about 5 miles (8 kilometers) from Salem Town. It was on the northern edge of Salem Town. Salem Town was the other main area of Salem. Salem Town was closer to the Atlantic coast. It was a port. It was a busy city. It had a lot of trade, businesses, and ships. About 1,500 people lived in Salem Town. About 500 people lived in Salem Village. Today, Salem Village is called Danvers. Several original buildings still stand. There's the house of Rebecca Nurse, which is a museum, and the remains of a church.

Vocabulary

hysterics (hih-STER-iks) fits of uncontrollable laughter or crying

disease (dih-ZEEZ) sickness

despair (dih-SPAIR) sadness

FLASH FACT!

There were many tests to identify witches. One test was to dunk the accused in water until they confessed.

TITUBA: They have to blame someone. We just have bad luck.

PATIENCE: I'm not a witch. I've never spoken with the devil. I've never harmed another person. Why is this happening to me?

TITUBA: It's happening to a lot of people. It's not fair. It doesn't make any sense.

PATIENCE: These silly little girls are taking over this town.

TITUBA: They're going around town acting like they're afflicted. They yell. They say **specters** are following them around.

Vocabulary

specters (SPEK-turz) ghosts

FLASH FACT!

Two dogs were executed for witchcraft.

PATIENCE: No one questions them. But they question us. How can I prove I'm not a witch? People believe what they want to believe.

TITUBA: Betty Parris and her cousin accused me. Who accused you?

PATIENCE: Ann Putnam accused me. First, she accused my older sister. Then, she pointed her finger at me.

TITUBA: I heard she's accused 62 people of being witches.

NARRATOR: **JOHN BARROWE** *visits another girl,* **MARTHA SMART***, next. She is also not feeling well.*

JOHN: I heard you've been sick.

MARTHA: I've had fevers. I've had stomach pains. I see a monster in my dreams.

JOHN: How often do you see this monster?

MARTHA: I see him after I have a deep sleep. Sometimes, I wake up screaming. My uncle says that I **babble**.

JOHN: This sounds like what Betty Parris and Abigail Williams are going through.

MARTHA: My uncle said I'm **bewitched**.

JOHN: Who is the witch attacking you?

MARTHA: The first name I can think of is Patience Dod. The second name is Tituba. Since I'm thinking those names, they must be witches.

JOHN: Are you accusing them?

MARTHA: All the other girls are accusing them. So, they must be witches.

Vocabulary

babble (BAB-uhl)
to say nonsense words

bewitched (bih-WICHD)
being under a witch's spell

FLASH FACT!

Mostly poor single women were accused of being witches.

ACT 2

NARRATOR: **PATIENCE DOD** *and* **TITUBA** *have been arrested and are in jail.*

PATIENCE: They're supposed to give us a trial.

TITUBA: It doesn't matter. The trials aren't going to be fair. We don't have many rights. We can't have **lawyers**. We can't have **witnesses**. We can only question our accusers.

PATIENCE: None of this seems right.

TITUBA: How did you get jailed?

PATIENCE: It's all because of Ann Putnam. My sister was on trial. Ann was acting strange. She screamed and called my sister a witch.

TITUBA: Then, what happened?

PATIENCE: I tried to help. I went to my sister. Then, Ann called me a witch. Next thing I know, I'm being dragged to jail. Can you believe that?

Vocabulary

lawyers (LOI-urz) people who study the law and defend those accused of a crime

witnesses (WIT-nis-iz) people who provide proof that something is or is not true

FLASH FACT!

Court trials for the accused witches were quick.

TITUBA: Defending people accused of being witches makes you an easy target.

PATIENCE: Ann is an evil little girl. People think we're doing the devil's work. But lying is the devil's work.

TITUBA: Even husbands have been jailed for defending their wives.

PATIENCE: Salem Village is not a safe place.

TITUBA: This jail isn't safe either. Four people have died here.

PATIENCE: It's horrible here. Our cells are **cramped**. There aren't any windows. It's cold and dark. It's smelly.

TITUBA: We're given so little food and water.

PATIENCE: It's also expensive. Can you believe we have to pay to live in this dump? We even have to pay for our **leg irons**.

TITUBA: What are you going to say in court tomorrow?

Vocabulary

cramped (KRAMPD) crowded

leg irons (LEG EYE-urnz) prison chains worn on legs

FLASH FACT!

Those found guilty of being witches were put to death.

PATIENCE: I don't know. I want to fight for my **innocence**. I want to say I'm not a witch. But so many people who have done that have been hanged.

TITUBA: If you refuse to answer questions, then they'll stone you to death.

PATIENCE: What are you going to do?

TITUBA: I'm telling them what they want to hear. I'm going to say, "The devil came to me and made me serve him. I didn't have a choice. Please help me."

Vocabulary
innocence (IN-uh-suhnts)
not being guilty

FLASH FACT!
Tituba was bullied. She confessed and accused others.

PATIENCE: You're going to admit to being a witch?

TITUBA: Yes. I'll have to stay in jail. But it's the only way to stay alive.

PATIENCE: We can't win.

NARRATOR: *People come from far and wide to watch the trials. The accused are questioned. Witnesses* ***testify****. The afflicted girls throw fits. They pull their hair. They beat their chests. Many of the accused women are found guilty. They are hanged. After several weeks, things quiet down. There are no more trials or hangings. One day,* **JOHN BARROWE** *speaks with* **MARTHA SMART***.*

JOHN: What happened in court that day?

MARTHA: I was just copying Ann Putnam. Ann was the **ringleader**. We all followed her lead. When she screamed, we screamed. When she fell to the floor, so did we.

JOHN: So, you lied?

MARTHA: I was just going along with the other girls. I didn't mean for anyone to get hurt.

JOHN: People died because of what you girls did and said.

BLOOPERS
HISTORICAL MISTAKES

The people of Salem got caught in panic and fear. But they still held trials. They applied the power of the law. That said, experts think the Salem witch trials were a mistake. They think a lot of women died for no reason. The trials allowed for "spectral evidence." This refers to dreams and visions. This is not real evidence. It shouldn't be used to order people's deaths. Cotton Mather was a minister. He warned against using spectral evidence. His father was Reverend Increase Mather. Increase Mather was the president of Harvard University. Increase said, "It were better that 10 suspected witches should escape than 1 innocent person be condemned." There was a lack of proof in the trials. In 1693, the hysteria started to end. Trial evidence was found to be false. On January 14, 1697, people honored all the innocent people who were killed. People started apologizing for their part in the trials.

Vocabulary

testify (TES-tuh-fye) to give evidence in court

ringleader (RING-lee-dur) the boss

FLASH FACT!

The accusers often thrashed around in the courtroom.

MARTHA: It all happened so quickly. Things got out of control. People were listening to us for the first time in our lives. What we said actually mattered. I liked the attention.

JOHN: What did you think was going to happen in court? You should've known things were **serious** then.

MARTHA: Adults were pushing us to accuse people. There was so much pressure. I didn't want to do it anymore. But it was too late.

JOHN: Why didn't you just tell the truth?

MARTHA: I had to keep going. If people found out I lied, then I would've been punished.

JOHN: The governor stopped the trials. There were too many deaths. Plus, his wife was accused of being a witch.

MARTHA: Thank goodness! The witch hunt is over!

Vocabulary
serious (SEER-ee-uhs)
not joking

FLASH FACT!

Most of the accusers were girls under 20 years old.

EVENT TIMELINE

- **1542:** The English government passes the Witchcraft Act of 1542. This is England's first witchcraft law. It makes the crime punishable by death.
- **1627:** Reverend Richard Bernard is in England. He wrote a book entitled *Guide to the Grand-Jury Men*. It's about prosecuting witches. It's used by the Salem judges.
- **1628:** John Endecott arrives in Salem Town, Massachusetts, with about 100 settlers. He becomes governor.
- **1638:** A small group settles outside of Salem Town. The area becomes Salem Village.
- **June 15, 1648:** Margaret Jones is the first to be executed for witchcraft in Massachusetts Bay Colony.
- **October 8, 1672:** Salem Village separates from Salem Town.
- **June 1688:** Reverend Samuel Parris arrives in Salem Village. He becomes the first minister.
- **1688:** Ann Glover works for the Goodwins. The daughter, Martha, acts strangely. She accuses Glover of witchcraft. Glover is executed in Boston.
- **January 1692:** Abigail Williams and Betty Parris behave oddly. A doctor tends to them. He states that witchcraft is the cause.
- **February 25, 1692:** Mary Sibley suggests making a witch cake to determine if Abigail and Betty are being affected by witchcraft. Flour was mixed with the accused's pee. The dough was shaped into a small cake and baked. Then it was fed to a dog. If the dog acted oddly, then the person is a witch. In this case, the dog acted fine.
- **February 1692:** The first accusations of witches in Salem Village begin.
- **March 1692:** The first examinations by judges begin.
- **May 1692:** First trials begin.
- **June 2, 1692:** Bridget Bishop goes to court. She's the first to be tried and convicted of witchcraft. She's sentenced to death.
- **June 10, 1692:** Bridget Bishop is hanged at Gallows Hill. This is the start of the executions.
- **October 29, 1692:** Governor William Phips orders the arrests to stop. He releases many of the accused from jail.
- **January 1693:** Several women are pardoned after being found guilty. This means they are innocent. Governor Phips says they cannot be executed.

CONSIDER THIS!

TAKE A POSITION! There were several possible causes for the Salem witch trials. One is that the girls were just bored. Another is that cold weather caused them to act oddly. A third cause could be poisoning. Learn more. Find out other causes. Which one makes sense to you? Argue your point with reasons and evidence.

SAY WHAT? Explain how the women in the witch trials were treated unfairly. What rights did women have at the time?

THINK ABOUT IT! How are the witch trials like peer pressure? Have you experienced peer pressure? If so, describe the experience. Also, describe your feelings. Explain why peer pressure is bad.

Learn More

Holub, Joan, and Dede Putra (illustr.). *What Were the Salem Witch Trials?* New York, NY: Grosset & Dunlap, 2015.

Marciniak, Kristin. *The Salem Witch Trials.* Ann Arbor, MI: Cherry Lake Publishing, 2014.

Schanzer, Rosalyn. *Witches: The Absolutely True Tale of Disaster in Salem.* Washington, DC: National Geographic Society, 2011.

INDEX

ABOUT THE AUTHOR

Dr. Virginia Loh-Hagan is an author, university professor, and former classroom teacher. She wrote a 45th Parallel Press book about witches. She lives in San Diego with her very tall husband and very naughty dogs. To learn more about her, visit www.virginialoh.com.